The African
AMERICAN Dilemma

THE
AFRICAN AMERICAN DILEMMA

BY

KHALID EL BEY

DEYEL PUBLISHING COMPANY
1818 SOUTH SALINA STREET STE. 5,
SYRACUSE, NEW YORK [13205]

CREATIVE RESEARCH SOCIETY
SYRACUSE, NEW YORK

ISBN: 1-4392-3565-1

Printed 2009

For information: www.khalidelbey.com

Cover illustration by Khalid El Bey

Published by
DEYEL PUBLISHING
1818 South Salina Street Ste. 5, Syracuse, New
York [13205]

CREATIVE RESEARCH SOCIETY
Syracuse New York
Printed in the United States of America.

CONTENTS

DEDICATION

I would like to dedicate this book to the many people who work in the struggle and to a few others who do what they can to assist: Khaliph Bey, Schym Bey, Supremiss Bey, Brandon Clark (Namaan Bey), Kevin Schoon, Ame Donkor, Omar Senior, Sean Hamilton; My Stars: Jarez Slater-Bey, Nadia Amani Bey & Saif Ahad El Bey; Java Clemmons, Sharif Bey, Freedom Torrence-Bey, Eric Glover, Divad Sanders, Jason Malone, Sondra Denise Roberts, David Rufus; My Mother & Sisters (Lisa, Venus, Lakea), My Brothers (Bad Man, Rama, Quincy), Bob Harrison, Ed Buford, Charles Pierce-El, Timothy Jennings-El, Steve Coker, Walt Dixie, Julius Edwards, Linda Littlejohn, Margie Gantt, and to the many who are not mentioned here.

PREFACE

The African American Dilemma is the work of Khalid El Bey, author, public speaker, politician and community activist. The purpose of this book is to assist the reader in identifying the possible cause(s) of the cultural confusion, ignorance and intolerance that has been the personality of American society for over two hundred years.

It was while taking a psychology course that I became aware of this underlying issue. This new awareness has inspired me to share with you my idea(s) for how we, as a society can improve. This book should be read by all who are affected by this issue, this dilemma, regardless of race or nationality. While the title suggests African Americans, there are many around the world that are a part of this or a similar struggle. *The African American Dilemma* faces this issue head on.

FORWARD

For centuries, African Americans have struggled with identity. Other cultures have labeled African Americans as lazy, inferior, and even animalistic. Not only have these labels been invented by other cultures in view of African Americans, but African Americans also have had distorted perceptions of themselves at times. These negative connotations have manifested in the form of rap music, racial profiling, lack of respect displayed in urban communities, and the continuous struggles of inequality within the workforce.

The African American Dilemma introduces a plausible cause as to why many of these perceptions exist today. Bey begins with a historical preface written by William (Willie) Lynch dating back to 1712. Lynch's doctrine proposed a methodology for domesticating Negro slaves which he professed to have a full proof controlling mechanism for hundreds of years. As highly noted by Bey, the primary purpose for Willie

Lynch's principle was to ensure that Negro families would be completely severed. Breaking the natural string of independency and creating a form of dependency was Lynch's way of guaranteeing success.

Bey draws a strong correlation between psychology and the teachings proposed by Willie Lynch. In order to create dependency, the mind and behavior of the slave had to be altered. Behavior is programmed through genetic manipulation or environmental influences. Bey speaks about what is deemed the most significant stage in a child's development, birth to 16 years of age. He mentions that the adolescent stage is a crucial phase for youth, who struggle to establish an identity. This is why parental involvement is imperative. If the family structure is broken, it is difficult for an adolescent to reach full potential.

The African American Dilemma explains that the degenerative cycle within the African American communities is a result of a certain personality pattern. This pattern or behavior is described as manner in which a person has difficulty acclimating to their environment.   The book does not place a stigma on African Americans.   It simply proposes a psychological theory for the conditioning that has taken place for hundreds of years.

The African American Dilemma is an extremely important book because it heightens our awareness for social change. It offers a psychological explanation for the issues exhibited by African Americans. What makes this book so powerful is because it challenges the responsibility of every American who contributes to the ill conditioning of mental processes. In order to overcome psychological destruction, everyone must be accountable, alleviating categorization and labeling. African Americans must learn to break the generational stronghold of Lynch's teachings and hold steadfast through societal issues that exist in order to make their destiny come to fruition.

- ***Roxanne Slater,***
  Ph. D. Candidate, Psychology
  MPA, Public Administration
  BA, Sociology

INTRODUCTION

When one takes the time to reflect on the reported aspirations of our founding fathers of this great nation, one can't help but wonder: what happened? If freedom, justice and equality are the principle concepts of our nation and if this great American experiment was a test of our willfulness to share in the responsibility and to compromise to assure that these three ideas together remain our chief cornerstone, then to date, we have failed miserably.

Efforts made during the civil rights movement in the 60's has lead the way in the attempts to eliminate bureaucratic racism. Many new opportunities have now surface for not just African Americans, but for all other minority groups, and in November 2008, America witnessed history with the election of our nation's first President of color; but how far have we really come?

If I was at one time very prejudice against Asians, but changes in the laws of the society within which I lived forbade me from openly expressing my dislike for Asians, have my negative thoughts of Asians really changed, or have I simply suppressed them? What good are my words if my every action is a contradiction? American society, like many societies around the world, suffers from the worse type of dis-ease: prejudice and selfishness, fueled by fear and ignorance. Once you've mixed this dis-ease with a survival of the fittest capitalistic type thinking, what you have is intellectual and moral anarchy.

I believe that the first step towards dealing with this condition is to identify its cause, for only in the identification of its cause can we began to understand its nature. Such an understanding could eventually lead us to the discovery of a "cure". I speak of this dis-ease as "it", because "it" has appeared to have taken on a life of its own. I also speak of this "it" as a condition, an illness or a plague, because it has infected the minds and hearts of many for well over twenty decades. It is my hope that this small contribution will assist the many who have made efforts thus far in the eradication of this terrible condition.

- *Khalid El Bey*

Author

ACKNOWLEDGEMENTS

I would like to thank Roxanne Slater for agreeing to write the forward for this work. I would also like to thank the following individuals who lent me an ear during the writing of this book:

Schym Ali El Bey, Joseph Bryant and Professor Ronnie Mather, who's Intro to Psychology class inspired this writing.

CHAPTER 1
What Dilemma?

What is the African-American dilemma? There are many who are probably attempting to figure out "is there in fact a dilemma and if so, can a solution to this dilemma be determined?" To people who are on the outside looking in, and by this I am referring to cultures outside of that of the African-American, the idea is that African-Americans are lazy, emotionally dramatic and to some, inferior; even genetically inferior or animalistic. They, the African-Americans, are creators of music that is characteristically sexists and violent. They are criminals who destroy neighborhoods, communities, and entire cities. It has been argued by some that criminal behavior is genetic and that African Americans, males in particular, have a tendency towards criminal activity. It is believed by some that African-Americans can't be trusted; that the women are loud, obnoxious, and lacking in self-esteem; and that the men are thieves who constantly fantasize about white women. This public distrust of African-American men could not have been made more apparent than it was during the 2008 presidential election here in the United States of America. Never before in history has there ever been such an attempt made to discredit and/or assassinate the character of a presidential nominee. Never before in the history of presidential rallies have there ever been statements made like "terrorist", "he's a Muslim" or worse, "kill that nigger"; at least not since the election of Abraham Lincoln. What is the African American dilemma? Do not even the most progressive African-Americans escape such stereotypes? Are all African-Americans guilty until proven innocent? Let us take a look at this situation from the African-American perspective.

To the average African-American, America is the land of the free, depending on the color of your skin. There are many African-Americans; men in particular, who feel that they are at a disadvantage,

President-Elect Barack Obama depicted as Osama Bin Laden during the 2008 Presidential election. Title: Barack Hussein Obama: Once a Muslim, always a Muslim. Photo courtesy of www.freepublic.com/focus/f-news/1755649/posts

President Abraham Lincoln depicted as an Indian April 6, 1852. Photo courtesy of www.docsouth.unc.edu/church/stanford/stanform.html

particularly in regards to finding employment. African-American women express concerns about what they term "a double whammy"; being African-American and female. In America, African-American men travel about with apprehension, for fear of being racially profiled while driving or sometimes even while walking down the street. African Americans equally have distrust for white Americans. African American men and women constantly speak of the discomfort they feel when entering a room full of white Americans. African Americans say that when entering a room full of white Americans, they feel as if the white Americans are judging them, which makes them apprehensive and uncomfortable. African Americans admit being more comfortable when being pulled over by an African-American police officer, and uncomfortable when pulled over by a white police officer. A white person on the other hand, instead of feeling discomfort when pulled over by an African American, feels superior regardless of if he is a police officer. But let's not only look at this dilemma from a cross-cultural perspective; let's also consider how we as African-Americans view ourselves.

Many African-American men view African-American women as emotionally dramatic, opportunistic, gold digging sex objects. Many African-American women view African-American men as lazy, horny, untrustworthy, and undependable dogs. From this standpoint, the way in which we view ourselves and the way in which we are perceived by others don't appear to be too different.

In one respect white America and other cultural groups in America view the African-American as a burden. They view the African-American as an inferior, who complains much, but does very little to improve his condition. The African-American complements this way of thinking by ultimately feeling and therefore acting inferior and dependent. The African-American men and women then further validates this judgment made on them by others, by lashing out at, fighting with, selling out, and/or killing one another.

One could argue that such behavior is not displayed by all African Americans, nor is such behavior confined to African-American culture, but that it may also be experienced within European and other cultures. Science attributes this type of superior vs. inferior behavior to Charles Darwin's theory of Natural Selection or "survival of the fittest". [1] This same theory, racist in its intent when applied to humans, speaks of natural selection based on heritable or genetic traits. [1] Some argue that such a theory breeds in people a total disregard for their fellow man. Is Darwin's theory 'the cause' of the natural instinct for survival in humans? I don't think so.

The word **dilemma** is defined as: any difficult or perplexing situation or problem. [2] I think you'd agree that the above qualifies as such.

CHAPTER 2
The Root Cause

To properly assess and understand this perplexing situation we would need to go deep. How deep you ask? Very deep. Let us begin with the recorded history of the African-American. From the European perspective, today's African-American is a descendent of slaves who were brought from Africa to America by way of the middle passage or trans-Atlantic slave trade. During this time period African men and women from sub-Sahara Africa were stripped away from their families and their homeland, taken to a land that was unfamiliar and forced to live in the worst of conditions.

Sketch of slaves tied together and lead through a grassy field.
www.timewake.us/Slavery/scourgeofslavery22.jpg

Reportedly, some of the white slave masters lived in fear of being overpowered by their slaves, due to the slave's very dominating appearance. There were also concerns for the safety and chastity of white women. In 1712 a man by the name of William Lynch, a British slave owner in the West Indies, was invited to the colony of Virginia to teach his methods for domesticating the Negro to slave owners there. The term "lynching" is derived from his last name. The following is his speech (quoted almost in its entirety) on the banks of the James River in 1712 Virginia:

"Gentlemen, I greet you here on the bank of the James River in the year of our Lord one thousand seven hundred and twelve. First, I shall thank you, the gentlemen of the Colony of Virginia, for bringing me here. I am here to help you solve some of your problems with slaves. Your invitation reached me on my modest plantation in the West Indies, where I have experimented with some of the newest and still the oldest methods for control of slaves. Ancient Rome would envy us if my program is implemented. As our boat sailed south on the James River, named for our illustrious King, whose version of the Bible we Cherish, I saw enough to know that your problem is not unique. While Rome used cords of wood as crosses for standing human bodies along its highways in great numbers, you are here using the tree and the rope on occasions. I caught the whiff of a dead slave hanging from a tree, a couple miles back. You are not only losing valuable stock by hangings, you are having uprisings, slaves are running away, your crops are sometimes left in the fields too long for maximum profit, you suffer occasional fires, and your animals are killed. Gentlemen, you know what your problems are; I do not need to elaborate. I am not here to enumerate your problems; I am here to introduce you to a method of solving them. In my bag here, I HAVE A FULL PROOF METHOD FOR CONTROLLING YOUR BLACK SLAVES. I guarantee every one of you that if installed correctly IT WILL CONTROL THE SLAVES FOR AT LEAST 300 HUNDREDS YEARS. My method is simple. Any member of your family or your overseer can use it. I HAVE OUTLINED A NUMBER OF DIFFERENCES AMONG THE SLAVES; AND I TAKE THESE DIFFERENCES AND MAKE THEM BIGGER. I USE FEAR, DISTRUST AND ENVY FOR CONTROL PURPOSES. These methods have worked on my modest plantation in the West Indies and it will work throughout the South. Take this simple little list of differences and think about them. On top of my list is "AGE" but it's there only because it starts with an "A." The second is "COLOR" or shade, there is INTELLIGENCE, SIZE, SEX, SIZES OF PLANTATIONS, STATUS on plantations, ATTITUDE of owners, whether the slaves live in the valley, on a hill, East, West, North, South, have fine hair, course hair, or is tall or short. Now that you have a list of differences, I shall give you an outline of action, but before that, I shall assure you that DISTRUST IS STRONGER THAN TRUST AND ENVY STRONGER THAN ADULATION, RESPECT OR ADMIRATION. The Black slaves after receiving this indoctrination shall carry on and will become self refueling and self generating for HUNDREDS of years, maybe THOUSANDS. Don't forget you must pitch the OLD black Male vs. the YOUNG black Male, and the YOUNG black Male against the OLD black male. You must use the DARK skin slaves vs. the LIGHT skin slaves, and the LIGHT skin slaves vs. the DARK skin slaves. You must use the FEMALE vs. the MALE. And the MALE vs. the FEMALE. You must also have your white servants and over- seers distrust all Blacks. But it is NECESSARY THAT YOUR SLAVES TRUST AND DEPEND ON US. THEY MUST LOVE, RESPECT

AND TRUST ONLY US. Gentlemen, these kits are your keys to control. Use them. Have your wives and children use them, never miss an opportunity. IF USED INTENSELY FOR ONE YEAR, THE SLAVES THEMSELVES WILL REMAIN PERPETUALLY DISTRUSTFUL. Thank you gentlemen." [3]

TO BE SOLD, on board the Ship Bance Island, on tuesday the 6th of May next, at Apley Ferry; a choice cargo of about 250 fine healthy

NEGROES,

just arrived from the Windward & Rice Coast. —The utmost care has already been taken, and shall be continued, to keep them free from the least danger of being infected with the SMALL-POX, no boat having been on board, and all other communication with people from Charles-Town prevented.

Austin, Laurens, & Appleby.

N. B. Full one Half of the above Negroes have had the SMALL-POX in their own Country.

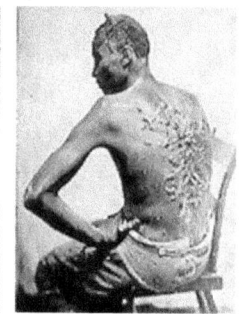

Photo courtesy of keepinitreal.squarespace.com

To add further insult to injury, Willie Lynch went on to say:

"First of all we need a black nigger man, a pregnant nigger woman and her baby nigger boy. Second, we will use the same basic principle that we use in breaking a horse, combined with some more sustaining factors. What we do with horses is that we break them from one form of life to another that is we reduce them from their natural state in nature. Whereas nature provides them with the natural capacity to take care of their offspring, **we break that natural string of independence from them and thereby create a dependency status**, so that we may be able to get from them useful production for our business and pleasure, for fear that our future Generations may not understand the principles of breaking both of the beast together, the nigger and the horse. We understand that short range planning economics results in periodic economic chaos; so that to avoid turmoil in the economy, it requires us to have breath and depth in long range comprehensive planning, articulating both skill sharp perceptions. We lay down the following principles for long range comprehensive economic planning. Both horse and niggers is no good to the economy in the wild or natural state. Both must be BROKEN and TIED together for orderly production. For orderly future, special and **particular attention must be paid to the FEMALE and the YOUNGEST offspring**. Both must be CROSSBRED to produce a variety and division of labor. Both must be taught to respond to a peculiar new LANGUAGE. **Psychological and physical instruction of CONTAINMENT must be created for both**. We hold the six cardinal principles as truth to be self evident, based upon the following the discourse concerning the economics of breaking and tying the horse and the nigger together, all inclusive of the six principles laid down about. NOTE: Neither principle alone will suffice for good economics. All principles must be employed for orderly good of the nation. Accordingly, both a wild horse and a wild or natured nigger is dangerous even if captured, for **they will have the tendency to seek their customary freedom, and in doing so, might kill you in your sleep**. YOU CANNOT REST. They sleep while you are awake, and are awake while you are asleep. They are DANGEROUS near the family house and it requires too much labor to watch them away from the house. Above all, you cannot get them to work in this natural state. Hence **both the horse and the nigger must be broken**; that is **breaking them from one form of mental life to another. KEEP THE BODY TAKE THE MIND!** In other words **break the will to resist**. Now the breaking process is the same for both the horse and the nigger, only slightly varying in degrees. But as we said before, there is an art in long range economic planning. **YOU MUST KEEP YOUR EYE AND THOUGHTS ON THE FEMALE and the OFFSPRING** of the horse and the nigger.

Photo courtesy of http://www.earlyamerica.com/review/
winter96/slavery.html

A   brief   discourse   in   offspring development will shed light on the key to sound economic principles. Pay little attention to the generation of original breaking, but **CONCENTRATE ON FUTURE GENERATION**. Therefore, **if you break the FEMALE mother, she will BREAK the offspring in its early years of development and when the offspring is old enough to work, she will deliver it up to you, for her normal female protective tendencies will have been lost in the original breaking process**. For example take the case of the wild stud horse, a female horse and an already infant horse and compare the breaking process with two captured nigger males in their natural state, a pregnant nigger woman with her infant offspring. Take the stud horse, break him for limited containment. Completely break the female horse until she becomes very gentle, where as you or anybody can ride her in her comfort. Breed the mare and the stud until you have the desired offspring. Then you can turn the stud to freedom until you need him again. **Train the female horse where by she will eat out of your hand, and she will in turn train the infant horse to eat out of your hand also**. When it comes to breaking the uncivilized nigger, use the same process, but vary the degree and step up the pressure, so as to do a complete **reversal of the mind. Take the meanest and most restless nigger, strip him of his clothes in front of the remaining male nigger, the female, and the nigger infant, tar and feather him, tie each leg to a different horse faced in opposite directions, set him a fire and beat both horses to pull him apart in front of the remaining nigger. The next step is to take a bull whip and beat the remaining nigger male to the point of death, in front of the female and the infant. Don't kill him, but PUT THE FEAR OF GOD IN HIM, for he can be useful for future breeding."** (end quote) [3]

The breaking of a slave.

From the African American perspective, these methods for instilling fear, for mind manipulation and control has evolved into the racial profiling, suppression, and socio-political injustices perpetuated by the police and other political powers throughout this country.   Are the African-Americans just whining? Should the African-Americans stop dwelling on the past, get over it, and move on?   Stephen Oates in his book, Portrait of America, Volume 1, 9th Edition, states: "This type of dehumanizing treatment was a part of the process by which merchandise was selected. It was also a part of the psychological process that attempted to 'strip away' the self-respect and sense of identity of the Africans." [4] Let's look at this matter from a much deeper perspective.

CHAPTER 3
The Effect

In his address, Willie Lynch spoke specifically about reversing the mind of the slave. What psychological effect did slavery have on the African-American? Psychology is defined as the scientific study of behavior and mental processes.[5] The word psychology comes from the roots *psyche* which means "mind", and *logos*, meaning "knowledge or study". [5] It is safe to say that Willie Lynch's intent was to alter the behavior and mental processes of the slaves. Behavior is defined as: the aggregate of the responses or reactions or movements made by an organism in any situation. [2] In other words, behavior is anything a person does under any given circumstances; when we're hungry, we eat; when we're sleepy, we sleep; when we're afraid…well, you get the picture.

Environment or Nurture

Are the behaviors displayed by African-Americans genetically or environmentally influenced? To answer this we would have to take a look at what scientists (psychologist) call **sensitive periods**. Sensitive periods are marked by a time when children are more susceptible to particular types of environmental influences. Events that take place during a sensitive period can permanently alter a child's course of development. [5] For example, if a woman drinks or smokes during the first trimester of her pregnancy the unborn fetus will be adversely affected, resulting in birth defects and possibly even stillbirth. For a child to develop normally certain events **must occur** during a sensitive period. A child may even have impaired language abilities if as a baby he or she doesn't hear normal speech regularly. [5] The human brain has nerve cell fibers that receive incoming messages from other nerve cells. These nerve cell fibers are called dendrites. In order for one nerve cell to receive a message from another, a *synapse* or a connection point between the two nerve cells over which the messages pass must develop.   Newborn babies have fewer dendrites and synapses than adults, but during an infant's first three years of life millions of connections between dendrites occur every day, and so early learning environments literally shape an infants developing brain. [5] In an environment like that of a slavery and/or poverty, developing children suffer from various levels of perceptual, intellectual, or emotional deprivation, resulting in a lasting damage to their social, emotional, and cognitive (mental) development.[5] What psychological effects do you think slavery had on developing African-American infants? I believe Willie Lynch had the answer. As mentioned a little earlier "*For a child to develop normally certain events **must occur** during a sensitive period.*"

Poverty in New Orleans 2007. Photo courtesy of
www.daylife.com/photo/08Kjcw7eST7im

According to recorded history slaves
were not allowed to learn to read or
write. If anyone was caught attempting
to teach a slave to read or if a slave was

caught reading, the person who was caught teaching a slave and/or the slave would be killed. According to Willie Lynch the "stud" or male slave, while important because of his is laboring abilities, was not the suggested point of focus. It was the female slave who was most important for she was the producer of the stud or male slave. Willie Lynch stressed the importance of focusing on the mother and the offspring. This was because in most instances the mother is the nurturer and teacher of the infant; if the mother has no mind, her child will have no mind.

Arrested Development

The actual sensitive period in a person's development is from birth to 16 years of age.[5] To give you an example of how sensitive the mind of a child is let's take a look at a child between the ages of two and seven years old. Children around this age generally lack the ability to determine words from the objects that these words represent. [5] In other words, to a two-year-old, if you call me a dog, I must be a dog. This confusion regarding words and the objects they represent is hardly ever corrected in infancy, and so this same confusion is carried into adolescence and even adulthood. This is why name-calling has as much of an effect on adolescents and young adults as it does on a two-year-old.

Adolescence is the most trying and confusing time period in a person's development. Transitioning from childhood to adulthood, the number one question with which a teenager is concerned is "Who am I? Establishing an identity is the most important task during this stage in life. "Adolescents or teenagers must work to develop a consistent identity out of their talents, values, life history, relationships, and their culture". [5] But if a child doesn't have family or environmental encouragement to assist in the developing latent talents; if she has no value for being told that she was a dumb, lazy, good for nothing nigger; if the history that he is taught of his family and his people tells him that they were nothing but slaves and that before they were slaves, they were savages running and hopping around like animals in the jungle; if their families were purposely destroyed and all they've ever witnessed were failed relationships; if her culture had been erased from historical record? What type of self-respect or dignity is this person expected to have?

CHAPTER 4
Products of the Environment

Emancipate: [latin] ēmancipāre, ēmancipāt- : ē-, ex-, ex- + mancipāre, **to sell, transfer**.[2]

"The Black slaves after receiving this indoctrination shall carry on and will become self refueling and self generating (slaves) for HUNDREDS of years, maybe THOUSANDS."

Are you free? What is it that characterizes freedom? A good job; I nice house or car; your right to vote? According to the doctrine mentioned in chapter 2, once indoctrinated, the African Americans would remain indoctrinated for hundreds, maybe even thousands of years. What effects could such indoctrination have on a developing mind? There are many African Americans who believe that they are free. One scientist argued that "unfamiliarity causes or produces limited understanding or a limited ability to perceive 'what is really there', and that most ideas have little meaning for someone until that someone experiences that idea".[5] To clarify the previous statement, the scientist was simply stating that people are inclined to doubt anything that is unfamiliar to them; that in order for a child to realize that fire is hot that child must be allowed to be burned. When someone or some thing has altered your consciousness they have equally effected your perception. Perception is the mental process of organizing sensations into meaningful patterns.[5] Sensations (or experiences) that are not already stored in one's long term memory will be viewed as unfamiliar and therefore unimportant while lodged in one's short term memory. Ideas or experiences which are not stored in one's long term memory will lack meaning (for him or her) and will naturally be discarded.[5] "How a person views the world is greatly influenced first by family, cultural, and environmental restrictions, and second by one's personal experiences".[5] When speaking of family filters or restrictions I am referring to a family's ideals or customs, which are usually shaped by that family's culture. When you add to the previous two (filters), the effects of environmental filters, a person's perception could be quite narrow. These filters or restrictions are certain behavioral boundaries within which a certain family, culture, or nation says a person should operate. These boundaries restrict or confine a person to a particular type of behavior, which in turn affects a person's world view or how they view the entirety of a given situation ("*behavior is anything a person does under any given circumstance*"). Familial, cultural and environmental standards affect a person's ideas of success, failure, right, wrong, legal, illegal, what's valuable, what's lacking in value, etc. A person's behavior cannot be accurately assessed absent an understanding of its cause. An understanding of the cause for certain behaviors could reveal motivations. Motivations refer to the dynamics of behavior or the ways in which our actions are initiated, sustained, directed, and terminated.[5] Initiated meaning why and how an action begins; sustained meaning reasons for the duration of an action; directed meaning the manner in which an action is carried out and the reasons for its direction; and terminated meaning why and how an action ended (usually because the desired goal was achieved or deemed unreachable). Many motivated activities begin with an internal deficiency or need. A person who feels that they are not living up to a particular cultural standard may be driven to do whatever is necessary including break the rules in order to achieve said standard. (Read my other book called "The Key to Character" for an explanation on the effects of family, cultural and environmental standards on the developing personality.)

African American male strip- search in an alley in Oakland, California. www.yannone.org/BlogPics/StripSearch.jpg

There are three types of motives: primary motives which are internal biological needs such as the need for food, water, air, etc.; stimulus motives which expressed the need for stimulation and information; and secondary motives which are based upon learned needs, drives and goals (like the need for a job, a college degree or certain types of companionship).[5]   A person's drive to achieve a particular goal will be affected by the incentive value or the goal's appeal beyond its ability to fill a need. [5] By this I mean that a person may be motivated by more than the idea of working to earn money in order to buy food; motivation could also be the idea that the work that they do may bring some other long-term benefit, like popularity for example. Some goals are so low in incentive value, that they may be rejected even if they meet an internal need. Certain goals can motivate people absent an internal need; an example of this is the wealthy person who destroys a competitors business in order to have a monopoly. This is a secondary or learned motivation acquired through a process called operant conditioning, where the promise of reward is the cause of a certain behavior.[5] Operant conditioning is equally caused by a threat of punishment; where a person avoids certain behaviors for fear of being punished. [5] The above are examples of primary (biological) and secondary (learned) motives. Certain learned fears, anxieties, ideas value, etc., help to shape the developing personality. Personality is a person's unique and relatively stable behavior pattern and refers to a person's way of thinking, behaving, and expressing their feelings. Personality traits refer to the most typical of one's behavior under a given circumstance. If a child while being raised, is condition to think and act in a certain way, his behavior under certain circumstances would become predictable.

If an experiment was conducted where a person who was hungry had to choose between satisfying his hunger and reading a book, what do you think this person do? What would you do? Is the outcome of this situation not predictable? Would not the person's behavior be predictable?

How would one categorize the thinking of a person who would reject a certain goal even though the goal satisfies an internal need? If at one point in the distant past you were denied the opportunity to learn; if when you had a son you told him to never look a white person in the face; if your a son told his son that he would only go so far in life because he was a Negro; and this son in turn passed the same ideas of inferiority, dissatisfaction and hopelessness on to his son, would the latter's behavior not be predictable?

Social Engineering

Thousands of years ago in the days of the hunter/gatherers, people would move and/or live in small groups, primarily because of limited food resources. These groups would travel from one environment to the next in search of animals to hunt for food, but soon a change in weather or seasonal conditions, and sometimes even the sensing of danger by the animals would make the animals scarce and so, finding food would sometimes become nearly impossible. [6] The women (who were usually the gatherers in ancient times) soon discovered that the planting of seeds into soil would in time produce edible vegetation; this discovery marked the beginning of agriculture. [6] The ability to grow food increased over time, resulting in a surplus of food and the ultimate attraction of lots of people. [6] This ability to grow food provided a sense of ease, thereby reducing 'the need' for hunting. One could easily discerned from this situation that an increase in resources could mean an increase in population; that people will naturally attract to where there exists an abundance of resources.

In the late 1800s and early 1900s, African-Americans were denied respectable employment, if they were allowed to work at all. The introduction of the welfare program during the Great Depression here in the US would change the social welfare of this nation for ever. African Americans, who were unable to work in those times, naturally saw the welfare program as an opportunity to acquire the resources they needed to care for their families.

In the 1950s and 60s Americans witnessed one of its most violent periods of racial conflict and inequality. We are now in the year 2009, just 41 years after the assassination of Dr. Martin Luther King, and there are some who wonder why many African Americans (women in particular) are not only recipients of the welfare system, but appear to be hopelessly dependent on it. As mentioned early-on, even in the earliest of times, any person desiring to survive will attract to where ever there appears to be an abundance of resources. A surplus of resources reduces "need", and so <u>a person's motivation is equally reduced.</u> Is three hundred and eighty-nine years of conditioning expected to be overturned by an 'idea' of racial equality and equal opportunity that has surface (realistically) only within the past 30 years?

Willie Lynch mentions that "*if the nigger woman was taught to eat out of their (the slave master's) hand, when her child grows, she will teach her child to do the same.*" He also mentions that "*if you break the FEMALE mother, she will BREAK the offspring in its early years of development and when the offspring is old enough to work, she will deliver it up to you, for her normal female protective tendencies will have been lost in the original breaking process.*" He further stated (in a part of his speech not displayed in this book) that "*if trained right, the nigger woman would become the 'gatekeeper', protecting the white man from the dangerous nigger male. The Black slaves after receiving this indoctrination shall carry on and will become self refueling and self generating (slaves) for HUNDREDS of years, maybe THOUSANDS.*"

Male slaves forced to stand in the back, while female slaves were kept close to slave masters.

As you can see Willie Lynch's methods were full proof, for still today African American women continually deliver their children up to the social services department and sell the fathers of their children to the state family courts, all in the name of public assistance.

Existential Therapy, which suggests that merely being in the world creates deep conflicts for people, says that every person lives in their own private world (mind), and possessesaninnateneedtocreatemeaning for their life.[5] To not create meaning or purpose for one's life could be quite tragic for anyone. Imagine the tragedy in the mind of a person who attempts, but fails to satisfy many of the sometimes unreachable and illusory familial, cultural or environmental standards. Most adults are still attempting to satisfy the identity crisis they encountered in adolescence (unsuccessfully). This idea suggests that many adults, regardless of their age or ethnicity, are still (emotionally) adolescent.

Genetics?

Is the African American male who breaks the 'rules' in an attempt to provide for his family a criminal? Understand that today there are different types of survival: economic, social, political, as well as literal (life) survival. "People naturally strive in the only ways that they perceive are available to them."[5] What is the expected behavior of a person who has been told, in one way or another, that they were not worthy of life's gifts, or that the general consensus is that most people who are like him (young,

African American, and male) will be arrested and/or have a criminal record, or be in jail or prison, or worse, be dead by a certain age? Is not the behavior of such a person under these circumstances predictable?

PHOTOBUCKET.COM

Is it possible that these kinds of thoughts haunting the private world (mind) of such a person could create a sense of urgency in regards to survival? I mean, his 'purpose' (to acquire a criminal record, be in prison or dead) has already been defined for him. What becomes his (or her) motivation? His private world becomes a world without boundaries; where the need for discovering purpose, which is essential to the securing of one's identity, is replaced by a desperate need to stay alive socially, economically, etc. What do 'you' think the African American dilemma is? Are the opinions that people of other cultures have about African Americans true? Is it possible that cultural restrictions and a questionable historical record could have impaired the vision or perception of our judges? Is it possible that years and years of conditioning have caused the various judgments made about African Americans to become true?

CHAPTER 5
The Diagnoses

A personality disorder is defined as: a maladaptive personality pattern. Maladaptive behavior is characterized by behavior that makes it difficult to adapt to the environment and meet the demands of day-to-day life. [5]

Now, there will be many African Americans who will be offended by what I am implying. They will argue and/or complain that I am saying that the African American is psychotic and that I am painting a negative picture of African Americans, but I don't think that I would be able to paint a worse picture of us than society has already. The African American dilemma is indeed a psychological one. If one would consider all that has been stated in this book thus far, what other conclusion could you have drawn? Most African Americans, due to years and years of conditioning, struggle to find their place within American society.

This qualifies the diagnoses as maladaptive, and therefore psychological, and not lazy or genetically inferior or criminal. American society has done a job on the mind of African Americans for hundreds of years, yet it expects the African American to acquire intellectual, emotional, social, economic, and political autonomy in a relatively short period of time (or at least that's the idea that American society promotes). But could the African American be expected to believe in America's plight for freedom, equal opportunity and equal justice, when what is reportedly a minority population makes up the larger percentage of the prison population? The Scientific Method, which is a method for testing the truth of a proposition by careful measurement and controlled observation, presents six stages for testing a proposition: 1) Making observations, 2) Defining a problem, 3) Proposing a hypothesis, 4) Gathering evidence/testing the hypothesis, 5) Publishing results, and 6) Theory building. [5]

As an experiment let us 'make an observation' and 'define a problem'. The observation is that the African American seems to struggle with the American capitalist survival of the fittest paradigm. The problem is that the African American is maladaptive. The 'proposed hypothesis' is incarceration. When one 'gathers the evidence of the hypothesis once tested' the 'published' results reveal that of a failing prison system. Though repeated time and again, state after state, the resultant theory is that the PRISON SYSTEM IS A FAILURE. Many who are released from prison are destined to return, because the prisons merely warehouses people and no longer provides any services that may help to improve the thinking of its inmates, which if it did, could help them to function more productively when released back into society.

If maladaptive behavior is considered psychological[5], why incarcerate an individual for a non-violent crime? Why not provide psychological therapy? In a national survey, nearly nine out of ten people who had sought mental health care said that their lives improved as a result of treatment. [5]

Some may argue that to provide therapy for so many would be an impossible headache; but to achieve success by improving the life of an individual could be worth the disappointment experienced in several cases where little to no progress is made. Research shows that 50 percent of all patients feel better after only eight therapy sessions. After 26 sessions, roughly 75 percent have improved. [5] The usual 'dose' of therapy is a one hour session per week. "This means that the majority of patients who underwent psychological therapy improve after only 6 months! Half of that number felt better in just two months." [5] Therapy could give a person a new perspective about themselves and their struggles, and could therefore give a person an opportunity to practice a new behavior. [5] As one could see, if the Scientific Method were applied to psychological therapy as a remedy, results would demonstrate its successes (particularly when compare to prison as a remedy), potentially reducing the chances of repeat 'maladaptive behaviors' that are probably unjustifiably characterized as crimes. In such a scenario, a sentence for a non-violent person would be from 6 months to 2 years (at the most), which would greatly reduce the tax burden on the American citizens. Though psychology provides a much better remedy than incarceration, a much better remedy would obviously be to prevent the crime from happening in the first place.

CHAPTER 6
An Educational Revolution

As mentioned in an earlier chapter, the question of identity begins in adolescence, so in regards to breaking the conditioning, where do we start?

Why is rap music so violent and sexist? Why is it so depressing? Why does it glorify superficial things like clothing, jewelry, cars and the like? Why does it appear to glorify the sale of drugs and promote murder? The answer might lie in the fact that most rap artist are teenagers and young adults. When you factor in the idea that the greatest challenge of a teenager is to establish an identity, and that the greatest desire of any human being is to establish meaning in their life, one would probably have a better understanding of the dilemma. To live in a society where being economically wealthy is the ultimate attainment; where violent programming and programming full of sexual content has a monopoly on television and the silver screen; where the areas in which you live are so economically, socially and politically desolate that people sometimes resort to stealing to survive; where the ethnic group to which you belong was violently brought to America, and is still today violently forced to live according to American custom, growing up in such a society could be quite the task for a young man who is trying to determine his worth as he travels the turbulent path from childhood to adulthood. Who is caring for the minds of the children? Most parents, like the prison system, merely warehouse their children; hardly ever or never spending an ounce of time investing in the minds of their children, yet wondering why the teacher calls and says that your daughter doesn't do any work, or wondering why she's failing her reading and comprehension class. Like many inmates in prison, children are left to do as they please; raised by television, music, and video games, and then released into society with no discipline, no education, and no sense of who they are. What's worse is that the children are then release into the care of adult teachers, most of whom are emotionally adolescent, and therefore sometimes incapable of handling an undisciplined child in the most professional manner. Imagine the difficulty of the middle school or high school educator. Hardly anyone in the entire building seems to be absolutely comfortable with who they are. Students constantly challenge the authority of teachers and administrators, because the students are capable of identifying a fraud; not because they're experts, but because they are guilty of fraud themselves, and so they are able to determine a sincere presentation from a phony one. Many of today's teenagers, regardless of ethnicity carry within them a sense of hopelessness. They act and speak as if life is at its end, and that they've accomplished all that is possible for them to accomplish.

It must be realized that the causes of the decreasingly low graduation rates or increasingly high – high school drop out rates are not academic, but psycho-sociological. [5] As human beings we are continually evolving and learning more about ourselves and nature as time progresses but just as the information that one receives in an educational environment improves or evolves, so to do the complications of such an environment. In an environment where the social dynamics outweigh the importance of academics, a newer approach to educating, not only for our students, but for our teachers may be the order of the day. Today's problem in our middle and high schools call for an educator with a background, not only in education, but in the social sciences as well. The development of a curriculum in Education, which includes disciplines in the social sciences, could produce an adult teacher capable of teaching, while also helping a student to cope with the social dynamics of a middle or high school environment. It is equally important that every culture be represented in middle and high school curriculums in the most positive way possible. A constant reminder of slavery might generate feelings of insignificance in the minds of African American students, negatively affecting one's thoughts of his people, his culture, and therefore himself. We must first improve our methods of educating the educators of our children in order to have a more harmoniously productive future.

CHAPTER 7
Freedom is Everybody's Job

Thus far the focus of this book has been on the psychological condition of the African-American. A continual discussion of the African-American dilemma could easily cause one to assume that the problem lies only within the African-American community. An understanding of (polar) opposites would provide one the ability to determine that if one extreme is greatly impaired, the opposing extreme must be inflated. Such is indeed the case with White Americans and other similar behaving cultures. In 1854 Philadelphia, Pennsylvania, a New York Tribune newspaper editor by the name of Horace Greeley suggested that the new 'White Man' (formerly referred to as red men, reportedly) declare an educational Revolution with the purpose of the deifying white Americans in the eyes of the Black slaves and the entire world. This suggestion would go on to fuel the doctrine of white supremacy. The labeling of 'white' people and 'black' people would represent two extremes: white implying life, pure, and intelligent; and black implying death, soiled, and evil. This idea of supremacy has been strategically embedded in the minds of white children for over a period of approximately 155 Years.

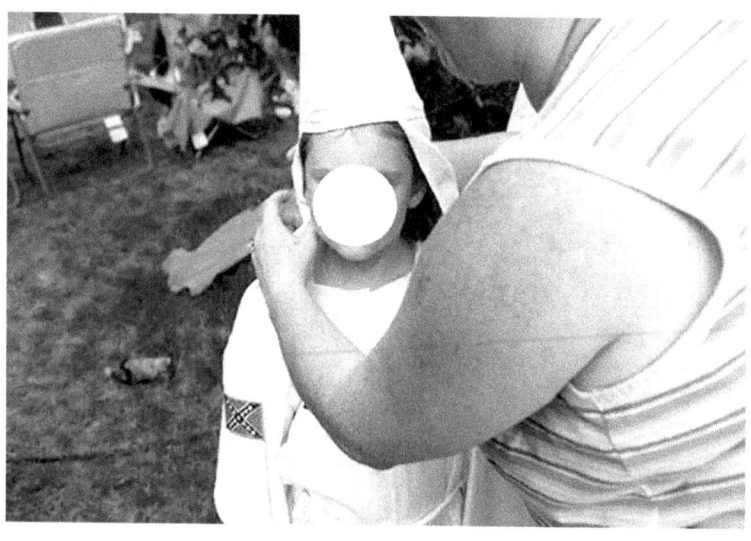

A mother dresses her young son in a Klansman robe.

What has to be understood is that the African-American feeling of inferiority could not exist absent a white American idea of superiority. White American children were taught that they were more beautiful, more intelligent, and more deserving or entitled, because their skin was fairer or lighter; but what is it that causes one's skin color to be fairer that another's?   African-Americans appear darker than white Americans because of melanin. Melanin is a class of compounds found in the plant, animal, and protista (microorganism) kingdoms, where it serves predominantly as a pigment.[7] Melanin absorbs harmful UV-radiation and transforms the energy into harmless amounts of heat through a process called "ultrafast internal conversion". This property enables melanin to dissipate more than 99.9% of the absorbed UV radiation as heat and it keeps the generation of free radicals at a minimum. [7] The most common form of biological melanin is eumelanin, a **brown-black** polymer of dihydroxyindole, dihydroxyindole carboxylic acid, and their reduced forms. [7] To clarify the idea communicated above: to possess high amounts of melanin, a class of compounds that are found in plants, animals and just about every other microorganisms that lives within nature, supposedly makes a person genetically inferior when compared to persons possessing lower amounts or no melanin at all? Absolutely not. The purpose of the previous statement is not to generate conflict, but instead to display that no part of this explanation on melanin suggest the inferiority of those who possess it; and also to display how idiotic and unscientific the idea of racial superiority is. There are some who may argue that the Willie Lynch letter was a hoax, and that there was no such person as Willie Lynch. Even if that were true, the conditions that are described in this letter are very real in the lives of every African American. White America has been conditioned through fear and false-education so to avoid a mixing of the races, an idea that is frighteningly reminiscent of the philosophies of Adolph Hitler. Though American society promotes the idea of a melting pot, it unconsciously and in some respects, consciously continues to promote white superiority and racial differences. As a result, African-Americans live a life full of self doubt; confined to a prison of worry and despair. This is not an attempt to point the finger of blame at white America, so let's be clear: the African-American walks into a room full of white Americans and assumes that he or she is being negatively judged, and this could very well be the case; but what is just as probable is that the idea of being judged is more imagined, than real. These thoughts held by African Americans cause them to become social isolates in a room full of people. The idea of African-American inferiority has been the biggest ball and chain, once again validating the words of William Lynch:

"*The Black slaves after receiving this indoctrination shall carry on and **will become self refueling and self generating (slaves)** for HUNDREDS of years, maybe THOUSANDS.*"

History reveals the fact that the African-American dilemma is greater than the African-American alone. It reveals that it is the responsibility of **every person** living in America who may have been guilty of knowingly or unknowingly perpetuating the greatest of conspiracies: the absolute (psychological) destruction of an entire nation, to make a sincere effort to improve intercultural relations. Though we may all share in the responsibility of righting the wrong by changing our perceptions; no longer categorizing entire groups, but instead learning to recognize its parts; the ultimate act of redemption is the task of the African American and him alone.

While American society continues to struggle with its ills, it would appear that the African-American has become her own overseer. Now is the time for the African-American to dig deep within herself, grab her slave master by the collar, and demand that she be set free. She must realize that though society is imperfect, she is the controller of her destiny; the determiner of her own fate. In my opinion, the exercising of the above methods towards liberation may prove beneficial in our quest to solve the African American Dilemma.

About the Author

Khalid El Bey attended Virginia State University in Petersburg, Virginia as a Social Work Major, and is currently pursuing a Bachelors Degree in Psychology at Empire State College in Saratoga Springs, New York. He has conducted independent research in history and law, and has studied non-traditional subjects, such as Astrology, Numerology and Qabala to name a few. He is the co-founder of the Creative Research Society, whose main focus is the re-education of the so-called African American and he is also an active member of a Al Moroccan Lodge, within the (Ecclesiastical) Ancient and Primitive Rite of Memphis & Mitzraim (freemasonry). Mr. Bey has lectured at a number of colleges and universities, as well as at a number of community events along the East coast and in the Midwest, and has spoken extensively about the true historical origins of man, mans personal identity and human relationships. Adding to his experience is his exploration of religion, esoteric psychology, Egyptian and Taoist alchemy. Mr. Bey is also very active in a number of community organizations in Syracuse, New York , where he's located. He is the Executive Director and Spokesperson for the Southside Community Coalition (a 501 C 3 non-profit organization), Spokesperson for Go Vote! (a socio-political organization) and even made a run for political office there in Syracuse in 2005.

"In order to change the world, all one has to do is change his mind," ....Khalid Bey.

Bibliography

Willie Lynch: The Making of a Slave. Online: www.thetalkingdrum.com/wil.html

Coon, D. & Mitterer, J. *Introduction to Psychology*. Thompson Wadsworth. 2007. United States.

Diamond, Jared. *Guns, Germs, and Steel*. W.W. Norton & Company. 1999. New York.

Definition of Melanin. Wikipedia free encyclopedia. Online. Darwin's Theory of *Natural Selection*. Wikipedia free encyclopedia.

Definition of *dilemma* according to Dictionary.com

Oates, Stephen B., Errico, Charles J. *Portrait of American, Vol. 1 (9th Ed)*. **Houghton Mifflin. 2007. New York.**

ENDNOTES

[1] Darwin's Theory of *Natural Selection*. Wikipedia free encyclopedia.

[2] Definition of *dilemma* according to Dictionary.com

[3] *Willie Lynch: The Making of a Slave*. Online: www. thetalkingdrum.com/wil.html

[4] Oates, Stephen B., Errico, Charles J. Portrait of American, Vol. 1 (9th Ed). Houghton Mifflin. 2007. New York.

[5] Coon, D. & Mitterer, J. *Introduction to Psychology*. Thompson Wadsworth. 2007. United States.

[6] Diamond, Jared. Guns, Germs, and Steel. W.W. Norton & Company. 1999. New York

[7] Definition of Melanin. Wikipedia free encyclopedia. Online.